Judge's Praise for Concrete Wolf
Chapbook Award Winner *Tumor Moon*

The push of the poems move you through this very unified work, the elegant and surprising mix of medical/scientific language blended with ordinary images, the emotion in each one. Each poem builds a crescendo you feel with the poet. There are a variety of forms to fit the specific subject of each poem that startle with both bluntness and eloquence. Not usually a fan of "medical/disease" themed works, this one won me with its cool honesty and deftly articulated sentiment without sentimentality. You are with this woman and her son as she navigates their experience. And the "conclusion" is that there is no "end point" in this endeavor, only a resolve to move forward. Each time I read this, I loved it all over again!

—Raphael Kosek, author of *Harmless Encounters*,
Winner of the Jessie Bryce Niles Chapbook Award

TUMOR MOON

TUMOR MOON

JENNIFER SAUNDERS

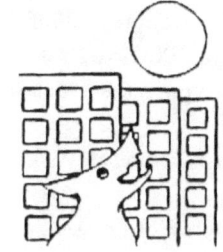

Concrete Wolf Press
Chapbook Award Series

Copyright © 2025 Jennifer Saunders

All rights reserved. No part of this publication may be reproduced, distributed, or transmitted in any form or by any means whatsoever without written permission from the publisher, except in the case of brief excerpts for critical reviews and articles. All inquiries should be addressed to Concrete Wolf Press.

Concrete Wolf Chapbook Award Series

Poetry
ISBN 979-8-9899488-8-8

Cover art: "Hunter's Moon Over Lawsonia, Wisconsin"
Copyright 2024 Steven Saunders Photography

Author photo: Denise O'Gorman

Design: Tonya Namura using Linux Libertine (text) and Rawengulk (display)

Concrete Wolf
PO Box 2220
Newport, OR 97365-0163

http://ConcreteWolf.com

ConcreteWolfPress@gmail.com

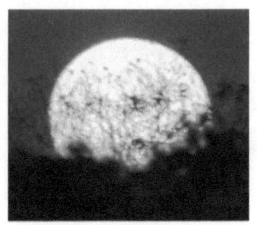

*For my son, who generously allowed these poems
to be published
with the one condition that his name not be used.
Your name doesn't appear here, but you know who you are.
These poems are for you.
Every letter of every word is for you
with all my love.*

Contents

Timeline / Memory	3
Ultrasound	5
Magnetic Resonance Imaging	6
Taking the Auspices	7
Surgical Biopsy	8
The Call	9
Welcome to Desmoidia	10
Watchful Waiting	14
Fruit Basket	15
Blood Draw	16
Medical Literature Abecedarian with Lyricism and Moments of Doubt	17
Watchful Waiting	18
Starting Treatment During Covid	19
An Apple a Day...	20
Winter Solstice with Desmoid Tumor	21
Starmap / Story	22
Tumor Moon	24
A Mother's Tarot	26
Idiopathic	27
We Turn to Hedylogos	28
Magnetic Resonance Procedure Screening Form for Patients	29
Between the MRI and the Meeting of the Tumor Board, He Feels His Tumor Tingling	30
Signal Change	31
First Day of School	32
Regularly Scheduled	33

Reading Homer While My Son Gets Another MRI   34
Memory / Timeline   35
Watchful Waiting   37
Desmoid Tumor Abecedarian
    with Honey and Flowers   38

Notes to the Poems   39
Gratitudes & Acknowledgments   43
About the Author   47

TUMOR MOON

Timeline / Memory

Recently, my datebook told me a story

    different from the one I've been telling myself

about my son's diagnosis. We careen

    in memory from one appointment to the next:

pediatrician-ultrasound-MRI-biopsy

    in the wingspan of a week.

But when I reconstruct the timeline,   gaps

    open   like tunnels. Seven days from

ultrasound to MRI. Blank calendar blocks

    before the regional hospital refers us

to the university hospital. Waiting

    for biopsy results. Time bends. I mis

-remember. Like when my hometown sledding hill

    where my brother and I spent our childhood

surprised me with how small it really is.

    I remember constantly skidding out of control,

sled lurching as we sped down winding tracks

    that tunneled through the bushes. Turns out,

it's a tiny little hill. Still, what I remember of those days,

    of those appointments,

is closing my eyes, ducking my head into my shoulders,

    and hoping the branches only graze me as I fly past.

Ultrasound

Inside the body,
the threshold
of softness.

Sound waves
reflected back
into boundaries
between time.

Each echo's return.

Magnetic Resonance Imaging

Electric current passed

      through coiled wires.

Muscle & bone pared
to protons.

Temporary magnetic field

      building inside you.

           Radio waves sent.   Received.

Signal strength, time lapse—
the scanned area of the body.

Rare earth metals in your veins.

Taking the Auspices

We're driving to the biopsy
when a starling darts
in front of the car,

flies into the windshield—
wet thunk—
then tumbles beneath the wheels.

I think: augury. Inauspicious,
according to the Romans,
the low flight of birds.

It certainly was for that bird,
I think. I think: let it be enough,
this accidental sacrifice to Asclepius.

This broken beak and plumage.
These entrails splattered for the gods.

Surgical Biopsy

the cells in question : suspicious

you : in a sleep-like state

the biopsy : whether cells are cancerous

    if the cells are cancerous :

                                        : wait

The Call

Such phone calls always catch you wrong
-footed. You're on the treadmill at the gym,

sweat slicking your palms.
Or you're at a poetry reading

when it vibrates its insistence.
Mid-game at the rink.

Never at home, never alone
in a room with a door you can close.

So you arrange your face when the doctor's number
lights up your home screen, raise a finger to signal

I have to take this. You seek out a corner,
scrim of privacy, press the phone to your ear.

You catch the words *biopsy results*,
catch *very rare*. You hear the doctor

tell you not to Google anything
before the appointment tomorrow.

Welcome to Desmoidia

I. Desmoid, from the Ancient Greek δεσμός (desmos)

A band, a bond. Imprisonment
or ligament. An infirmity.

Appearing twenty times
in the New Testament.

Mark used it to describe
a speech impediment.

Luke, to describe
a maimed woman.

Possibly wreath or fetter.
Also a spell or charm.

Mooring cable, door latch, yoke-strap.
Modern usage: relationship, connection.

Medical: tumor that develops
in the fibrous tissue of ligament and tendon.

II. May Also Be Called

Aggressive fibromatosis

    musculoaponeurotic fibromatosis

        familial infiltrative fibromatosis

            desmoid fibromatosis

                deep fibromatosis

                    hereditary desmoid disease

III. Theories of Formation

Mostly sporadic.
Mostly of unknown origin.

One theory: desmoids
are healing run amok—

fibroblasts that won't stop growing,
scar tissue transforming recovery

to damage like wine reverting to water.
A missed signal, beta-catenin

cataracting through the body
in a profusion of production.

So I say injury.
Blocked shot, why not:

my son turning his body
into the path of the puck.

Let's say he was up by one in the third,
let's say time was running down.

Let's say he held his ground.

IV. Histology

The tumor appears striking,

        a poorly circumscribed proliferation of cells

                      pink and plump
                      darkly staining
                      the final figure

V. Learning Curve

VI. Standard of Care: Watchful Waiting

They used to resect desmoids.
Excise from the body

the foreign body.
I wanted that—

for someone to take a knife
to my son.

Out with that dark moon
orbiting the future.

These days, it's *watchful waiting*—
data collection to monitor

the new object in the body's sky,
its uncertain trajectory.

Watchful Waiting

Monitor the tumor to see if it grows. Monitor the tumor to see if it grows.

Fruit Basket
> *Tumor sizes are often measured in centimeters or inches. Common food items that can be used to show tumor size in cm include: a pea (1 cm), a peanut (2 cm), a grape (3 cm), a walnut (4 cm), a lime (5 cm), an egg (6 cm), a peach (7 cm), and a grapefruit (10 cm).*
>
> —Cancer.gov

Many tumors grow slowly:
little peanut, little pea, wee
blueberry. Red currant, wild
strawberry, sweet seedless grape.
Terms
       of endearment, means
       of measurement.

Some tumors grow quickly,
fill orchards with their windfall.
What we're unable to can
will rot in the grass. The air thick
with fermenting fruit.

Slowly. Quickly. We don't know.
Monitor and measure,
weigh fruit on the scales.
I hold that plum in my hands
and feel for bruise and blight.

Blood Draw

We get the good nurse—
though this is pediatric oncology,
where every nurse is the good nurse—
but I mean the *really* good nurse,
my favorite nurse, the nurse
who remembers that blood draws
make my son faint so always reserves him
a reclining chair. The nurse
who guides his breathing like a midwife—
breathe in, breathe out,
breathe in, breathe out—
all through the first vial and the second,
and the third, then brings him orange juice
and lets him rest for as long as he wants.

      In the room next door,
a little girl needs an infusion
so they call in the clown.
He plays the accordion and tap dances.
Through the partition I hear the girl giggle,
then laugh. She doesn't cry.
The clown passes us by, tap dances
in other children's rooms.

Medical Literature Abecedarian with Lyricism and Moments of Doubt

Apophenia: a tendency to perceive meaningful connections
between unrelated things. My IVF, his
chronic condition. It's crossed my mind. The thing with rare
diseases is that each case draws its own map of the
edge of the observable universe, quasars redshifting.
Fibromatosis: benign infiltrating proliferations of fibroblasts
  and myofibroblasts.
Give me any handful of stars, I'll build you a constellation
homogeneous and hypoechoic and characterized by
insidious growth. Irregular borders infiltrate & intertwine.
Just because it's not malignant doesn't mean it can't
kill you one day. ("Death can result from
local effects," Kingston et al. informs me.)
Maybe the small lumps I've always had on my leg mean
nothing. Maybe meaningless, the embryonic years
  in cold storage.
Oncology and ontology are both a study of being.
Perhaps a single transposed letter means everything.
  Now it's a
question of drugs and dosage, a matter of monitoring.
Refractory diseases stop responding to treatment.
Stable and *stasis* don't mean cured.
The problem with chronic conditions—they're inherently
uncertain. Watch-and-wait, wait-and-see, the
visible spectrum of bodies earthy and unbound.
When observation fails, then what?
(Xie et al. notes that disease course is unpredictable.)
Yesterday, another MRI.
Zones of low signal intensity, distant and luminous stars.

Watchful Waiting

Q: Is hope a method of treatment?
A: It is not an entirely risk-free endeavor.

Starting Treatment During Covid

In the hinge between a summer
of open-air dining and falling

case numbers and the oncoming
winter of closed doors and stuffy

classrooms, we begin to compromise
our son's immune system. They

are the color of brick, his meds,
and I am told not to touch them

with my bare hands. My son
can touch them, raise them

from blister pack to mouth.
No matter if he absorbs

toxins through his skin
when he swallows his poison

in hopes of slowing the growth
of a tumor that at first

we thought was a bruise.
Now there's a box of chemotherapy

in our kitchen, stored away
from direct sunlight.

He is only just beginning, barely
into the first sheet of pills, and we sit

in this moment between seasons,
the sweet gum tree blazing red.

An Apple a Day…

He's eaten them for years
in all their sundry forms:

sliced with peanut butter.
Baked into a pie. Pureed.

Juiced. Jellied and jammed. Plucked
straight from his grandmother's tree

and barely polished on his tee shirt.
He's eaten them Granny Smith,

he's eaten them Pink Lady.
Empire. Fuji. Gala and Golden

Delicious. Peeled and cored.
A little bit bruised. Too firm

for his milk teeth, too soft
to survive his backpack.

In the locker room after the game.
Tart after tart after tart. Turn

-overs. Dried and stirred into oatmeal.
Years of them. Bobbed-for and candied,

stuck on a stick and dipped in caramel,
raw and cooked and quartered

he's eaten them and eaten them
and eaten them and no. It doesn't.

Winter Solstice with Desmoid Tumor

Disruptions to the supply chain delay delivery
of our son's Sorafenib, and we're down
to a day-and-a-half worth of meds
even though we called in the refill
with a week's worth of pills in the pack.

Now it's December twenty-third.
The year tilts towards light.
The doctor's office is closed tomorrow.
We've let our son run out of meds
for the holidays.

We haven't trimmed the tree
and the Lego we ordered is delayed.
We're waiting for the doctor to call.
We're waiting for the delivery truck.
We're waiting for the next MRI—
hoping for a little less light,
a little more shadow.

Starmap / Story

I told myself a story. There was a full moon.

    There was no moon. The stars

were unmappable. Nothing matched

    the celestial chart. Night sky.

Light pollution blurring my vision.

    Do astronomy textbooks go out of date?

Can I go back to nineteen-eighty-eight, Riddle Point,

    night sky still dark enough

to map? Plot the paths of the planets,

    the dark moon of the future.

Learn the constellations and the stories

    that named them. Orion's belt. The crab.

Dim, dimmer. Early spring, night sky, slow map

    emerging. First the arrow, then the archer.

Tell me a story, make me a myth. Seafoam me

    a winged horse upside down in the sky.

I told myself a story. It started with the North Star.

    I tried to use the stars to guide me.

Tried to find a polestar. I told a story.

There was a full moon. There was no moon.

There were the stars.

Major. Minor. Ursa.

Tumor Moon

Tumor as hunter's moon
riding the shorn field of the body,
beaver moon building its fibroblast dam.

We chart its course across months
of the vanishing solstice sun,
find our way by the light of the long night moon.
Wolf moon howling at our door.

If I could hold it, turn it in my hands
under the light of the full hunger moon,
would it feel like a rotting apple? A peeled plum?
Would it smell like sap and turned dirt?

Child, this is your orchard.
Worm moon: larvae and grub.
There are 7,000 species of earthworms,
one for each rare disease. Desmoid worm.
Desmoid moon blooming like wild phlox.
If I could hold it, would it bleed spring moon pink?
Full flower moon petaling itself into a bouquet.

Would it stain my hands strawberry?
False fruit sending out runners,
tumor unplucked and a thunder moon
raining down to flood field and stream.
Tumor spawning under the sturgeon moon.
If I could hold it, would it shimmer like roe?

Full tumor moon waxing,
exerting its gravity on the tides of our days.
Tumor as moon, tumor as tide, tumor as corn
before the threshing. The moon rises early,
stays long in the sky. Moon to harvest by.

Spoiled crop sown in the body.
The earth turns a year of moons, hunter
to harvest and hunter again. Hunter moon,
hunter tumor. Bow. Arrow. Quiver.

A Mother's Tarot
   for C

The Death card paired with the Moon
is just another way of saying watch and wait,
just another MRI on the calendar.

Death doesn't portend death
but transformation, the end of a phase.
We're cycling through the options,

eyeing the black new moon on your ultrasound,
bright-mooned tumor on your MRI.
Did I ever tell you, you were born

under a lucky star? I knew from the start:
you were a freshly minted coin.
Four of Pentacles, *merciful earth*, and listen—

you are within the walls of a strong castle.
I'll weave you a net with these nots:
not-malignant, not-metastasizing,

not-The Tower. Not today. Shuffle
through the leaves on your way home from school.
There's leftover Halloween candy and a flame still burns

in the pumpkin you carved by slicing away
what didn't serve your purpose,
cutting out everything that blocked the light.

Idiopathic

I think it was trauma from a hockey puck—
my son blocking a shot in some now-forgotten game.
My friend thinks it's high-voltage power lines,
lingering radiation from Fukushima,
heavy metals, *all this shit in the environment*,
she says, waving her hands.

The body, a poet once wrote, *is a black box.*
Who knows what waved that wand,
transformed muscle tissue to tumor.
Injury, electricity, magnetic fields.
Something in the soil
on his grandfather's farm.
Apples from some sprayed tree.

I told my friend my son keeps losing weight.
The meds steal his appetite,
but he can still eat noodles.
Now, each time we meet,
she brings me fresh ramen,
handmade and vacuum-packed
from the specialty shop.
I treasure these blocks of nutrition,
these calories I know he'll keep down.

They're wrapped in plastic.
They were made by strangers.
I put them in my son's body.

We Turn to Hedylogos

Because we can't be rid of you, O moon
that never sets, let us flatter you and fawn,
buy you off with trinkets and adorn
your dark side with sequins. We'll ply you
with baby-box mementos: first lock of hair, first tooth.
We'll bring you forget-me-nots and hawthorn
to make you forget us, smother you with charm,
smooth your orbital path with petals strewn

across your transit. We'll braid you daisy crowns
and train the crows to bring you shiny beads,
bracelets, and baubles. O apricot, O plum,
O date-sized swelling, let us beguile you down
to dormancy, lull lull lullaby you to sleep,
let us cajole you to quiescence, you mass. You lump.

Magnetic Resonance Procedure Screening Form for Patients
after Michele Bombardier and Tiana Clark

Have you ever been a	body part to be examined?
Are you wearing	claustrophobia?
Are you allergic to	examination?
Are you currently taking	braces?
Have you ever worked with	a previous reaction?
Have you ever been	a prior surgery?
Do you suffer from	details?
Have you ever experienced	a magnetic field?
Have you ever had	noise levels?
Are you	a brain clip?
Do you have a history of	electric currents?
Have you ever been injured by	your body?

Between the MRI and the Meeting of the Tumor Board, He Feels His Tumor Tingling

and the website tells me this could mean nothing,
or it could mean the tumor is expanding, impinging
on nerve, on blood vessel, could be tendrilling,
could be dendriting and helixing.

He's been so lucky, this child
with a mutation spiking his bloodstream.
If you had to get a tumor, I told him once,
you picked a good one.
As if there could be a good one. But listen—
I've spent years in these waiting rooms
and I'm telling you: there are good ones.
Locally aggressive but non-malignant
falls here like a blessing. The difference
between calf and neck an unmappable universe.

Now: a tingle like flesh fallen asleep.
For a week after the MRI, I am built of nothing
but waiting and the ruptured sky.
Watch and wait wears on me—
years of watch, years of wait, years
I wear like ragged butterfly wings.
He wears his beautiful bones, wears
his tumor with grace and forgetting
as if he knows the watched- and waited-for
storm will turn. He believes in the good horse
of his body, the lucky penny in his fist.

When again the MRI report reads *stable*, I am grateful
and guilty. How to carry this much grace?
Dragonflies, poppies, the thorned menace
in his body blossoming into this gentle stasis,
this morning that dawns & dawns & dawns.

Signal Change

Wither, then; wither and fade.
Dry like leaves in autumn, grow

brittle like frazil, like bleached
coral, like the unprotected bones

of the dead. Unwatered tree,
unfed stream, slow deforestation,

this blessed die-off. These
sloughed cells, this unswelling.

First Day of School

On a late summer morning that holds
the first intimations of the coming fall,

a boy gets on his bicycle and rides off
for the first day of a new school year

in a new school building.
He is wearing shorts, and either does

or does not care that people can
or cannot see the swelling on his calf;

he doesn't say (he's that age).
The boy has lived three years

with the tumor, has seen its starshape
shine on his MRIs, has swallowed the poison

that slowly shrinks the tumor
but does not vanish it. The boy

has learned to live with the side effects.
The boy has learned to live

with the tumor.
The boy's voice is beginning

to change (he's that age).
He is starting high school.

Watch him pedal his bicycle
down the road, watch the tumor

appear and disappear
with the muscle's each flex and release.

Regularly Scheduled

The mail comes—they've scheduled an MRI again.
I check my calendar, cancel a lunch,
    sign my son out of school.
I can hardly believe it's been
three months—already MRI time again.
The doctors need to measure his tumor's trend,
see if treatment has it under control.
I put away the mail. An MRI again.
It's scheduled for after lunch.
    He'll only miss half a day of school.

Reading Homer While My Son Gets Another MRI

I have seen into my son's body
too many times: X-ray and MRI, ultrasound.
Blood panel blood panel blood panel.
I know by heart the way he pales and faints,
the specific gravity of his buckling knees.

What I've learned: orange juice
and chocolate croissants revive him.
Play "Hockey's Greatest Goals" on YouTube
when the nurse can't find a vein. What he's learned:
don't watch the test tubes fill. Breathe—
the anticipation is worse than the experience.
We are striving for stasis, for constancy
        rather than cure.

His doctors tell me he can live a normal life
with a tumor like that. Provided stasis. Provided
constant monitoring of those shadow-cells transformed
into a pantheon of tiny gods that rule us. God of muscle,
god of mutation. God of iron and liver enzyme.
God of soft tissue, god of biopsy needle, god
of radio waves and the speed at which they bounce back.
God of mass and measurement and of anything but growth.

In some mythologies, a goddess
would slice out the tumor herself.
Would gnaw the flesh with her teeth
then lick the wound like a cat until it healed,
her saliva glowing silver in the moonlight.
In the old myths, her saliva would grant immortality,
or harden, perhaps, to a sheath of armor.

Child, forgive me. I'm no goddess.
I have no river to dip you in.
I have no shield to bequeath.

Memory / Timeline

I fly past the deer and the downed trees

    past fireflies hovering low on the grass

I fly past the start of evening and the clock tower

    chiming its you're-too-late chimes

rattling bats from their perches I fly

    past the bats with their toes specially designed

to relax in a locked position and wouldn't that

    be something to be at my most attached

while most relaxed secure even in sleep

    and bats really do sleep upside down

I fly past the rows of their bodies leathery

    like vanilla pods and I fly past

vanilla vines tendrilling up the clock tower

    I fly fruit-forward five-o'clock

and pour myself a glass of Malbec and my fingers

    are most relaxed when they're curled

around something pen coffee cup goblet stem

    wrist or rock I fly past midnight

past Orion past Atlas holding up the world

    and wonder if his shoulders are most relaxed

when holding that weight and look at the bats, look—

    their little feet clinging through their dreams.

Watchful Waiting

When the end comes it is not the end.
The treatment ended, the tumor remained.
Smaller. Not gone. Never gone.
Gone the pills, the vomiting.

The treatment ended. The tumor remains,
noontime star.
Not gone. The pills and vomiting
recede into memory

like stars at noontime. What does it mean
to seek uncertain stasis? Soon this too
will recede into memory,
this brief respite—

because we said *stasis* too soon.
Watchful waiting, monitor & measure,
bring an end to this brief respite.
Like the moon the tumor

sits watchful, waiting
in his unshielded body.
Bright tumor moon on his MRI illuminating
everything I can't protect him from,

not even his own body.
The tumor has grown again.
I can't protect him from this.
When the end comes, it is not the end.

Desmoid Tumor Abecedarian
with Honey and Flowers
*   for C*

Active surveillance, watch & wait,
between *indolent* and *locally aggressive*
comes tyrosine kinase inhibitors, comes
data collection, comes calculating the odds of
event free survival. Comes nausea, comes
fatigue, comes throwing up in the bushes and
going to practice anyway, comes still playing
hockey when even short shifts are too long.
(Honey, tell the coach when it's not going well.
It's okay to rest, honey.)
Invasive just another word for pushy,
just another word for back to the tyrosine
kinase inhibitors when the tumor
looms again like a full flower moon on your latest
MRI. April, and the cherry tree is in blossom,
narcissus littering the yard. April, and
our grape hyacinth is taking over,
profligate & proliferating like the not-
quiescent cells swelling your calf.
Regression is the goal, but I'll settle for
stasis. What I want
to tell you is that life was always
unpredictable—it's just more obvious now.
Variable clinical course just another way of saying
we'll figure it out as we go. There's no
x-marks-the-spot, no calendar's circled end date. But
yesterday it didn't frost overnight. Come May, we can set
zinnias. What I want to tell you, honey,
      is that something is always blooming.

Notes to the Poems

The poem "Ultrasound" is an erasure/collage of information found at https://www.nibib.nih.gov/science-education/science-topics/ultrasound.

The poem "Magnetic Resonance Imaging" borrows language from a description of magnetic resonance imaging found at https://www.fda.gov/radiation-emitting-products/medical-imaging/mri-magnetic-resonance-imaging.

The poem "Surgical Biopsy" is an erasure of information found at https://www.mayoclinic.org/diseases-conditions/cancer/in-depth/biopsy/art-20043922

In the poem "Welcome to Desmoidia" Section I, the phrase "develops in the fibrous tissue of ligament and tendon" is taken from https://www.webmd.com/colorectal-cancer/desmoid-tumors-facts. Section IV is an erasure/collage of the section "Histology of DTF" from the paper "Biology and Treatment of Aggressive Fibromatosis or Desmoid Tumor" by Keith M. Skubitz, MD, appearing in *Mayo Clinic Proceedings* Volume 92, Issue 6, pp 947–964, June 2017.

In the poem "Medical Literature Abecedarian with Lyricism and Moments of Doubt" the phrases "Death can result from local effects" and "Zones of low signal intensity" are taken from "Imaging of Desmoid Fibromatosis in Pediatric Patients" by Catherine A. Kingston, Catherine M. Owens, Annmarie Jeanes, and Marian Malone in *American Journal of Roentgenology* Volume 178, Issue 1, January 2002. The phrase "When observation fails" is taken from "Desmoid tumors in children: when wait-and-see becomes wait-and-treat" by Aaron Weiss and Douglas Hawkins in *The Lancet Child & Adolescent Health*, Volume 1, Issue 4, December

2017. The reference to Xie et al. refers to "Case report: A rare case of desmoid-type fibromatosis originating in the small intestine" by Xie, Junfeng et al. in *Frontiers in Medicine*, 31 October 2023, Volume 10. A map of the observable universe can be viewed at https://mapoftheuniverse.net/

Language in "Watchful Waiting" (2) is taken from "Is Hope a Method? Commentary on an article by Sylvain Brian, MD, et al.: 'Wait-and-See Policy as a First-Line Management for Extra-Abdominal Desmoid Tumors'" by Potter, Benjamin K., MD; Forsberg, Jonathan A., MD, in *The Journal of Bone & Joint Surgery*, April 16, 2014: Vol 96, Issue 8.

In the poem "A Mother's Tarot," the italicized language is from *Tarot Dictionary and Compendium* by Jana Riley.

In the poem "Idiopathic," the line "The body is a black box" is a modification of the poem title "Every Human is a Black Box" by Jeannine Hall Gailey.

"Magnetic Resonance Procedure Screening Form for Patients" is after "Aphasia Testing" by Michele Bombardier and borrows its form from "Equilibrium" by Tiana Clark.

In the poem "Signal Change," a T2W signal decrease in an MRI of a soft tissue tumor from one MRI to a follow-up MRI indicates that the tumor is becoming less viable.

In the poem "Desmoid Tumor Abecedarian with Honey and Flowers," italicized language is taken from "The Management of Desmoid Tumors: A joint global evidence-based consensus guideline approach for adult and pediatric patients" from the Desmoid Tumor Working Group.

You can learn more about desmoid tumors and the search for a cure at the Desmoid Tumor Research Foundation website: https://dtrf.org/

Gratitudes & Acknowledgments

I would like to thank Raphael Kosek for selecting this manuscript and Lana Hechtman Ayers at Concrete Wolf for publishing it. This manuscript sits in my heart more deeply than anything I've yet written, and I am ever grateful for your bringing it into being.

To my Frustration of Poets, always, for your unending support, love, and encouragement: Jamaica Baldwin, Michele Bombardier, Nancy Miller Gomez, Rebecca Patrascu, and Craig van Rooyen. What would these poems (by which I mean what would I) be without you? With an extra heaping of thanks to Nancy for the title.

To my Swiss Sisters near and far who received early drafts of many of these poems with tenderness and care: Theresa Bühlmann, Ruramisai Charumbira, Neria Moye, and Astrid Vangenechten.

To my Wellfleet sisters: Laura Gail Grohe, Amanda Oliver Hendricks, Chelsea Krieg, Eve Lyons, Katherine Perry, Rae Rose, Andrea Witzke Slot, and in loving memory of Fiona Bennett.

To Rachel Neve-Midbar. Buddelas forever.

To all the class- and workshop mates I've written with over the years sharing physical or electronic space, to the poets whose work inspires me, to my teachers and mentors past and present, thank you for sharing the writing life with me.

To the physical therapy team for SCB, in Bern, Switzerland, who first told my son: *that's not muscular.* Thank you. An das Physiotherapie-Team des SCB, in Bern, Schweiz, das meinem Sohn als Erstes sagte: *Das ist nicht muskulös.* Merci viu mou.

And last but never least to my family, anonymous all to protect the anonymity of one (but you all know who you are). For your love, support, encouragement, understanding of my absences both physical and mental, and for your all-around general amazingness. I love you. An Heidi, für alles und mehr.

To my brother, Steve Saunders, for so much more than the cover image. When we were kids, you'd take pictures of the clouds and I'd write in my diary and look at us now. I love you.

"Taking the Auspices" is for Reto Häni.

"The Call" is for Theresa Bühlmann and Neria Moye.

"Blood Draw" is for the nurses in the pediatric haematology and oncology department at the Inselspital in Bern, Switzerland. Every one of you is my favorite nurse. "Blood Draw" ist für die Krankenschwestern der Pädiatrischen Hämatologie/Onkologie im Inselspital in Bern, Schweiz. Jede von Ihnen ist meine Lieblingskrankenschwester.

"Idiopathic" is for Neria Moye.

"Reading Homer While My Son Gets Another MRI" owes a debt of gratitude to my 2022 Kenyon Summer Writers Workshop Raccoonteurs, especially Casey Catherine Moore.

"Memory / Timeline" is for Paul Tran, with deepest gratitude.

I would like to thank the following journals in which some these poems first appeared:

MIDLVLMAG: "Winter Solstice with Desmoid Tumor"

Salamander Magazine: "Starting Treatment During Covid"

About the Author

Jennifer Saunders is the author of *Tumor Moon*, winner of the Concrete Wolf Chapbook Contest, and *Self-Portrait with Housewife*, winner of the Clockwise Chapbook Competition (Tebot Bach, 2019). She is also the co-editor of *Stained: an anthology of writing about menstruation* (Querencia Press, 2023), a multi-genre anthology that breaks the silence surrounding the menstruating body. Jennifer's poems and reviews can be found in *Adroit, Chestnut Review, The Georgia Review, Literary Mama, Ninth Letter, Poet Lore, Salamander, San Pedro River Review*, and elsewhere as well as in several anthologies and craft books including *Masque Anthology* and *The Strategic Poet: Honing the Craft*.

Jennifer's poem "Crosswalk" was selected by Kim Addonizio as the winner of the 2020 Gregory O'Donoghue International Poetry Prize and appeared in *Southword*. Her poem "What If I Could Tell You Everything About Myself By Quoting Others?" earned an Honorable Mention in the Geneva Literary Prize judged by Sharon Mesmer. Jennifer is a multiple Pushcart, Best of the Net, and Orison Anthology nominee.

Born and raised in suburban Chicago, Jennifer now lives in German-speaking Switzerland with her husband and two children. A lifelong hockey enthusiast, she has taught skating in a hockey school in Bern, Switzerland, for over ten years and continues to drive her hockey-playing son to many, many ice rinks. She has seen some glorious moonrises and moonsets along the way.

www.ingramcontent.com/pod-product-compliance
Lightning Source LLC
LaVergne TN
LVHW041552070526
838199LV00046B/1927